ANOINTED PATHWAYS

A WOMAN'S MEMOIR OF GOD'S DISCERNING MIRACLES IN HER STRUGGLES

E. T. MULLONEY

TABLE OF CONTENTS

Part IV

COPING WITH LIFE'S ULTIMATE TESTS

DISCLAIMER

This memoir is a true account of events and facts as experienced and remembered by the author. However, in order to protect the privacy and identities of individuals involved, names and some identifying details have been changed. The intent is to respect the privacy and confidentiality of those who have played a role in the author's life. All efforts have been made to ensure the accuracy and honesty of the narrative while safeguarding the privacy of individuals portrayed herein.

TRIGGER WARNING

This book contains content that may be triggering for some readers. It includes scenes depicting sexual assault and explores themes of loss and grief. We advise readers to exercise caution and consider their emotional well-being before proceeding. If you or someone you know is struggling with similar issues, please seek appropriate support or counseling.

This book is dedicated to my ever-supportive husband, Patrick, who is the unwavering anchor of my life alongside God—a testament to you, my constant source of love, support, encouragement, and inspiration. Every page in this story of our life as a family is enriched by your presence, and our beloved fur baby, Tiggy boy, adds a special charm to our amazing story together. We are truly blessed!

INTRODUCTION: LET'S BEGIN

In the quiet moments before dawn, as the world lay shrouded in darkness, I found myself standing at the crossroads of faith and doubt. It was in those hushed hours when the night still held sway, where the veil between the ordinary and the divine grew thin, that I discovered the undeniable presence of miracles.

Imagine with me, if you will, the profound stillness of those early morning hours. The world was wrapped in a cloak of obsidian, a canvas painted with the deepest shades of night. The usual cacophony of life was hushed, and the weight of the unknown hung in the air. It was in these sacred moments I felt a connection to something greater than myself, a force that defied explanation.

Miracles, you see, are not the stuff of fairy tales or the lofty realms of ancient legends. They are the quiet whispers of hope in our everyday lives, the unseen hands that guide us when we stumble in the darkness. They are the moments when the improbable becomes a reality, and the ordinary transforms into the extraordinary.

In the heart of my story lies a testament to the unwavering belief in a power greater than ourselves—a belief that has been the steadfast companion of my journey. It's a belief that has been forged through trials and tribulations, moments of despair and elation, and the ebb and flow of life's unpredictable currents.

In *Anointed Pathways*, I invite you to walk beside me on the path of my life, where struggles and blessings are entwined and where the discerning hand of God guides me along a path illuminated by the most extraordinary of miracles. It is a story that transcends borders and touches the human spirit, for faith, divine intervention, and unwavering belief in God is not confined by geographical boundaries.

Our journey begins in the rugged mountains of the Philippines, a place where my mother and I lived without running water or electricity. Picture the towering peaks that loomed above us, their majesty both awe-inspiring and humbling. We carried water on our backs as we trekked through the mountains, the weight of our struggles etched into our very beings. I studied by the flickering light of a kerosene lamp that often threatened to extinguish in the gusty winds. Financial hardships were a constant presence in our lives, but through it all, we clung to the dream of education—a dream that was as unyielding as the mountains themselves.

Life, however, had other plans for us. As an adult, I would find myself in the Middle East, a land of scorching deserts and unfamiliar customs. The sun would blaze relentlessly, and the culture was vastly different from my own. It was there that I felt the weight of my responsibilities most acutely, burdened by the mantle of being the family's sole breadwinner. It was there that my faith in God became my refuge as I faced intense struggles, unfamiliar terrain, trauma, violence, and the challenges of an entirely different world.

Miracles would unfold in ways I could never have imagined throughout my life, and as you journey with me through the pages of this memoir, you'll witness the incredible moments when divine intervention turned the tide in my favor. *Anointed Pathways* is a testament to the resilience of the human spirit and the power of unwavering faith. It's a story that speaks to the universal human experience, reminding us of all that miracles are not reserved for a chosen few—they are woven into the fabric of our lives, waiting to be discovered.

So, I invite you to turn the page to delve into the chapters that follow. Reflect on your own experiences, struggles, and beliefs, for within these pages; you'll find moments of inspiration, loss, hope, grief, and profound insight. And as you do, may you be reminded that even in the darkest of nights, the dawn of miracles is just beyond the horizon.

Let's begin this extraordinary journey together, where faith and miracles intersect, where the human spirit soars, and where the power of belief can move mountains.

PART I

CHILDHOOD MIRACLES IN ASIA—A FOUNDATION OF FAITH

God's miracles are to be found in nature itself; the wind and waves, the wood that becomes a tree - all of these are explained biologically, but behind them is the hand of God.

— RONALD REAGAN

1

THE HAUNTED ROOM

Thank you for joining me on my journey through faith and resilience. This is where my journey begins. A small child in a small room facing terrors I would have to learn to deal with, faith in hand.

ECHOES FROM THE PAST

In the quietude of my childhood, amidst the bustling city of Manila, my life beginnings would be shaped by a haunting presence that would linger in my memories like a ghostly echo. This was a time of innocence, when I was merely a 3-year-old child, grappling with the complexities of life, a life shadowed by the separation of my parents. We had settled into a modest room in a worn-down building, the only place my mother and I could afford as we started on our journey through life, just the two of us.

The room itself was a stark contrast to the world outside. It was a small, cramped space devoid of warmth and light. Its walls held the secrets of countless lives, its air heavy with the weight of time. The musty odor that clung to the room seemed to seep into my very soul, a scent that lingers in my memory to this day.

From my small vantage point as a child, the room was always teeming with activity, a revolving door of people coming and going, their voices filling the air with an incessant hum. It felt busy, loud, and a stark contrast to the tranquility I yearned for.

One fateful night, as I lay cocooned in my bed, blissfully ignorant of the world's troubles, a subtle yet unmistakable sensation began to creep upon me. It started as a gentle rustling, as though the blankets were caressing my skin, their soft touch drawing me out of my slumber. But soon, the gentle touch transformed into an unnerving force, as if an unseen hand had taken hold of my ankles and was tugging me with an unnatural urgency.

Startled, my eyes snapped open, and my heart raced with fear. In the dimly lit room at the foot of my bed, a dark and grotesque figure loomed. Its form was indistinct, like a wisp of smoke, and it seemed almost translucent, ethereal in its nightmarish quality. I watched in terror as its hands clenched around my ankles, its ghostly fingers pulling and tugging at my fragile legs.

As a mere child, I knew instinctively that this apparition could not be real, for it defied the laws of nature and reason. Yet, its eerie presence filled me with dread. Questions flooded my mind: Who was this shadowy figure? What did it want from me? Would it harm me?

Confusion enveloped me, and I cried out in terror. My screams pierced the stillness of the night, a desperate plea for salvation from this malevolent specter. My mother, awakened by my frantic cries, burst into the room in a whirlwind of concern. She, of course, could not see the entity that tormented me.

Desperate to protect her child, my mother clutched the Bible tightly in her hands and pressed it against my trembling back. In a voice that trembled with resolve, she began to recite prayers of protection, rebuking the malevolent force that had invaded our sacred space. My tearfilled eyes never left the apparition at the foot of my bed as my mother's prayers intensified.

With a final, defiant gesture, I pointed towards the open door, indicating the sinister intruder's exit. The dark figure seemed to yield to my mother's unwavering faith and retreated into the shadows, fading into obscurity.

This terrifying episode became an almost nightly ordeal, etching a deep trauma into my psyche, one that would forever alter my relationship with sleep. My nights were plagued by fear, and I often wondered if I was losing my grasp on reality.

My mother, in an attempt to make sense of these disturbing occurrences, revealed a chilling detail about our room. She explained that the building had once served as a hospital, a place where life and death had intersected on countless occasions. We had chosen this place for its affordability, unaware of the lingering echoes of the past that haunted its walls.

THE FIRST SEEDS OF FAITH

It would be in that room that I would come to understand the power of faith and divine intervention in the face of darkness. These early encounters with the unknown would shape my unwavering belief in God, a belief that would become my steadfast refuge in the face of the many trials and tribulations that lay ahead on my path of resilience, healing, and faith.

At the tender age of three, I couldn't comprehend the world of dreams and nightmares, and the lines between reality and imagination blurred. I would wake up trembling, my heart pounding, and tears streaming down my face.

But there was one constant in those moments of fear and confusion: my mother's unwavering faith. She would rush to my side, her soothing presence a balm to my frightened soul. She would cradle me in her arms, and, in her gentle voice, she would recite Bible verses, sing hymns, and offer praises to God. Her stories about Jesus were like a beacon of hope in the darkness of our room.

I can still hear her soft and melodious voice as she taught me the verses that would become my refuge, especially Psalm 23. "The Lord is my shepherd; I shall not want (Emberley, 2021)." Those words became etched in my heart, a reminder that even in the midst of life's trials and tribulations, God is our protector, our provider, and our guiding shepherd. My mother's lessons gave me solace and the strength to confront the terror that plagued my dreams.

She would reassure me that all I needed to do when I felt scared was to say those verses out loud, and the malevolent presence that haunted my nights would flee. This was my first real experience of using faith to conquer fear, and it marked the beginning of a lifelong journey of spiritual growth.

Looking back, those early years were the first seeds of faith that were sown deep within my soul. They were the foundation upon which I would build my unwavering belief in God. It was through the darkness of those nights and the loving guidance of my mother that I began to understand the power of faith to bring light into the darkest corners of our lives.

LOOKING BACK WITH MATURED EYES

As I sit down to pen down the story of my life, I can't help but marvel at the journey I've taken, from a humble beginning on one of the mountainous islands in the Philippines to a life far from home in the Middle East. Looking back with mature eyes, I see my past as a tapestry woven with threads of faith, divine intervention, and unwavering belief in God.

Childhood, for me, was a stark contrast to the world I know today. Raised by a single mother, our modest home lacked the luxuries most people take for granted. I can still feel the weight of carrying that water, both physical and metaphorical.

My education was a precious dream, one that felt impossible to attain amidst our financial hardships in a third-world country. Yet, my mother instilled in me an unyielding faith in God and the power of education. She showed me to let faith and God be my guiding light through the darkest nights.

I was blessed to have my mother comfort me, assuring me that God was watching over us, even in the face of fear. Now, as an adult, I understand that those nightmares were symbolic of the challenges and adversities that would shape my life. They taught me resilience and the importance of holding onto faith even in the darkest moments.

Looking back, I realize that divine lessons were hidden within those childhood traumas. In a strange way, the dark figure prepared me for the uncertainties and fears I would encounter later in life. It taught me to confront my fears head-on and seek solace in my unwavering belief in God's protection. I would never be alone; He would always be by my side. My mother was preparing me for this.

Despite the hardships, both seen and unseen, I can now see how God's miracles were always at work in my life. There were times when we didn't know where our next meal would come from, yet somehow, provisions would arrive just in time. The winds that blew out our kerosene lamp also carried with them a whisper of hope, a reminder that even in the most challenging circumstances, God was there, guiding us along the path to a brighter future.

As I reflect on those early years, I'm filled with gratitude for the lessons learned, the strength gained, and the unwavering faith that carried me through. Looking back, I see how my childhood nightmares and my mother's teachings were essential building blocks that shaped the person I am today. They laid the foundation for the challenges I had no idea were ahead of me.

2

A SIX-YEAR-OLD LOST IN THE WOODS

I vividly recall that day when I felt my innocence met the unknown. It happened in the mountainside of the island province in the Philippines, where my mother and I had relocated after living in the rooming house. We moved there to take care of my ailing grandfather, as my mother was considered a "single mom," which was a taboo and a source of disgrace in our family back then.

As a child raised in the city, the mountainside was a captivating wonderland for me. The scent of wildflowers and the vibrant dance of dragonflies and butterflies had always enchanted me. On that particular day, with the sun high up in the sky, I was filled with glee as I chased these winged creatures, my feet carrying me deeper into the woods. The beauty of nature was mesmerizing, and the world around me was brimming with discoveries. My heart was light, and for a moment, the weight of our familial struggles was forgotten.

But then, like a scene from a storybook, the playful chirping of birds gradually faded into the distance, and the once-clear path became obscured. Panic surged through me. How had I let my fascination lead me so far astray? The towering trees around me seemed more menacing now, their shadows converging, transforming the forest into a labyrinth of uncertainty.

Tears welled up in my eyes as the realization of being alone in this vast wilderness hit me hard. I felt small, vulnerable, and deeply scared. My youthful innocence was shattered by the profound weight of my situation.

I was lost for what felt like an eternity, though it was probably only an hour or so. In this small community, everyone was familiar with everyone. My grandfather had put out a call and before too long, they were all searching for me. All I could hear were the birds chirping, the buzzing of insects, the high-pitched hum of cicadas, and the unrelenting heat of the sun bearing down on me.

I walked aimlessly, the tears streaming down my face as I cried out for help. But with every step, thorns from bushes scratching my skin, the unfamiliarity of the terrain only seemed to intensify. The warm tendrils of the sun bore down on me relentlessly, and my throat felt parched from both the heat and my anxious sobs. Hope was slipping away, and a sense of helplessness settled in my heart.

In that moment of fear and vulnerability, I couldn't help but pray. Despite my young age of six, I had already developed a deep faith in God, nurtured by my mother's unwavering belief. I had grown up with my mother teaching me Bible verses to say out loud and songs to sing when I was scared, whether it was because of nightmares or being lost in the woods. In that moment of uncertainty and fear, I found myself instinctively reciting those verses and singing those songs, feeling a profound sense of protection and companionship. I prayed for guidance and protection, and slowly but surely, I started to calm down. I felt a sense of peace. I just knew I would be okay. It was as if a reassuring presence enveloped me, reminding me that I was not alone and that there was hope even in the darkest of moments. I sat down on a pile of rocks and waited for help.

Just when it seemed that all hope was lost, a mysterious figure appeared in the distance. It was a silhouette of a local man, his identity recognized by the traditional garments he wore. His presence in that remote part of the forest was surreal, almost like a mirage. Though I couldn't communicate with him using the native dialect, the comforting smile he offered was universal. He approached me with a grace and kindness that transcended language barriers.

As he knelt beside me, he reached into a small flask and offered me water. The relief that washed over me as I sipped from the flask was palpable. It was a lifeline in that moment of desperation, quenching my thirst and soothing my parched throat. But it was more than just a physical rescue; it was a beacon of hope in a situation that had felt increasingly dire.

There was something uncanny about this encounter. Amidst the vastness of the forest, the chances of someone crossing my path, especially at the right moment when I needed help the most, felt like more than just a coincidence. It felt divinely orchestrated as if the universe itself had conspired to bring this kind stranger to my aid.

Eventually, the sound of distant voices reached my ears, and my mom found me, tears of relief streaming down her face. The family was shocked, later telling us that the pile of rocks they found me on would normally be filled with snakes hiding out. I had been kept safe. I had been protected.

That experience, though frightening, taught me a valuable lesson about the power of faith and the importance of staying connected to our roots, even in the face of adversity.

It was a small glimpse of the challenges and adversities that lay ahead in my journey, but it also served as a foundation for the unwavering belief in God that would guide me through the many struggles and hardships, I was yet to know I would encounter as I grew older. Faith would become my refuge once again as I navigated the unknown, always believing that with God by my side, I could overcome anything.

Once rescued and safely back in the embrace of my anxious family, the gravity of what had transpired began to sink in. While I had been lost for just an hour, that hour had felt like a lifetime. The wilderness had become both a terrifying and enlightening teacher.

As I sat with my family, recounting the ordeal, I couldn't help but reflect on the true power of the verses and songs my mother had instilled in me. In those moments of deep despair in the forest, they had been my anchor, my solace.

The words of the Bible and the melodies of those songs had not only soothed my fears but had also filled me with a sense of hope and resilience. It was as though they were a lifeline connecting me to something greater than myself. The same had happened in that rented room during those awful nightmares.

I couldn't shake off the feeling that someone, something beyond our earthly realm, had been watching over me during that harrowing experience. The encounter with the kind stranger in the forest, the inexplicable timing of his arrival, and the feeling of being cradled in the arms of an unseen presence all contributed to this profound realization. This experience laid the very foundation of my unshakable belief in divine intervention.

It was in this moment that I learned about faith—the kind of faith that assures you that you're never truly alone, even in your most vulnerable hour. I discovered that there is a spiritual dimension to our existence, one that transcends the physical world and reaches into the realm of the miraculous. It taught me that there are forces at work beyond our comprehension, guiding, protecting, and always present, even when we cannot see them with our eyes.

This ordeal in the woods wasn't just about a lost child finding her way back home; it was about a soul recognizing the hand of God in her life. It was about understanding that divine guidance is real and tangible, that it can manifest in unexpected ways, and that it's always there for those who believe. Even though I was but a child at the time, I felt a deep and profound connection to something much larger than myself—a bond that would only grow stronger in the years to come. This experience set the course for a lifelong journey of faith, resilience, and an unwavering belief in the presence of the divine in every aspect of my life.

Years later, I've often revisited that day, not just as a harrowing tale to recount to friends and family but as a profound and enduring reminder of the extraordinary power of faith. It was the first time in my life that I felt part of a larger plan, a tapestry that was still being woven by forces beyond our comprehension. This experience served as the cornerstone of my beliefs, the moment when I began to understand that there was more to life than what met the eye. It was a revelation that would change the course of my existence forever.

As I reflect on that day, I can't help but see it as a pivotal point in my spiritual journey. It was a day when the circumstances of our family's life in that remote island, facing the societal backlash of my mother's singlehood and grappling with the weight of my grandfather's declining health all converged to create the backdrop for this profound spiritual revelation.

In that moment, amidst the towering trees and under the unrelenting sun, I wasn't just a lost child in the woods but a soul being gently nudged toward the divine. It was as if God Himself had orchestrated the events leading up to that day, knowing that it would be a turning point in my life. It was a nudge—a divine invitation, if you will—that would shape the very essence of my existence.

I began to see that the challenges and adversities we faced as a family were not just random occurrences but part of a larger, intricate design. They were threads woven into the tapestry of our lives, each one serving a purpose in our journey of growth and discovery. It was a realization that brought a profound sense of comfort and purpose, knowing that even in our most difficult moments, we were not alone. God's hand guided us, shaped our destinies, and revealed Himself in the most unexpected places.

That day in the forest was the beginning of my deep-seated belief in the divine. It marked the start of a lifelong quest to explore and deepen my faith, to seek God's presence in every aspect of my life, and to trust that even when I feel alone, even when I feel defeated, there is a greater plan at work—one that continues to unfold, revealing its beauty and purpose in ways we may not always understand. It was a moment of awakening, a glimpse into the boundless possibilities of faith, and the assurance that, indeed, we are all part of a greater plan, a tapestry still being woven by the hand of the divine.

This experience sowed the seeds of faith in divine guidance deep within me. It taught me that when I think I cannot go on when life is at its worst, there can be a glimmer of light, a helping hand extended when you need it most. It instilled in me the unwavering belief that God is always with us, guiding us through our trials and tribulations and that sometimes, the most extraordinary moments are the ones where faith and the miraculous intersect.

3

HIGH SCHOOL MIRACLES

High school corridors can be pathways to classrooms of calculus and literature, but for me, they were also tunnels leading to profound self-discovery and spiritual enlightenment. In those years, the worn-down tiles underfoot were the silent witnesses to my secret battle with dysmenorrhea—a struggle that would unexpectedly fortify my faith in the divine.

As I traveled those halls, their linoleum tiles scuffed and worn from years of countless footsteps, I recall the air was thick with the scent of textbooks and body odor. There was a constant chatter of students echoing in my head. For most, just a typical school day, but for me, those corridors held a deeper significance.

With every onset of my menstrual cycle, I braced for a maelstrom of pain. The agony twisted through me, so intense at times that the world would spin and fade to black, leaving me to awaken to hushed whispers and concerned stares. "She's fainted again," they would murmur. I remember the consuming embarrassment, the hot flush of shame that burned brighter than the midday sun as I lay there, vulnerable, on the ground. The whispers of my peers felt like a stinging breeze against my skin.

Each month, I was met with pain I could barely tolerate. Doctor after doctor could find nothing wrong with me. At that time, uneducated male doctors wouldn't give a second thought to my female anatomy and what could be lingering within. My mother and my cousins were afflicted with similar pain, so I suffered, convinced it was a family history.

The high school I attended had a big program, and everybody was preparing for it. Visitors, teachers, and superintendents from other schools would be invited to watch the Reserve Officers Training Corps (ROTC) performance. They are tasked with training and developing high school students in the rudiments of Military Service in order to produce capable Armed Forces of the Philippines reservists. This was a big deal for all of us.

This happened to land on the first day of my period! Even before the program started, I was weak, light-headed, and in pain, but I still continued. I felt my knees begin to shake. I prayed to God and tried to focus on my breathing. The room began to fade, and that was the last thing I remembered. I had lost consciousness during the drill.

Then, the unthinkable. They had called my mother! Her panicked voice, piercing through the quietude of my brief respite from pain, announced to all the source of my frailty. I wished I could dissolve into the earth, escape the prying eyes that would surely see me as nothing more than the girl who crumbled under her own body's betrayal. This was high school, and all of my peers saw me at my most vulnerable.

In these moments of pain and humiliation, the high school corridors became more than just passageways; they witnessed my resilience. I remember the sensation of the cold tiles underfoot as I struggled to my feet, the world still spinning. The stark contrast between the bustling school life around me and the private battle I was waging within my own body intensified the isolation of the moment. I truly wanted to disappear.

There would be yet another monumentally embarrassing moment for me during my high school years. Each month, when my body tried to deal with the excruciating pain, it would often affect my bladder and bowels. Being educated about this as an adult, I now know these are all connected. I didn't have a bus that went to and from school, so I would walk the same path with other classmates. One day, the pain was too much. I was sweating through my uniform, and the bowel cramps were more than I could deal with. We were in a residential neighborhood, and there were no businesses I could run into and use the bathroom. Soon enough, I realized I had no choice. I had to knock on a stranger's door and ask to use their bathroom.

I would spend an hour in their home with diarrhea. A young girl with a soiled uniform, blood stains, sweat, with no running water or toilet tissue. I continued to pray for healing and strength. I would thank the lady for letting me use her home, although she made it clear I wouldn't be welcome again. I would have to walk home to change my clothes.

High school was both my crucible and my sanctuary. In its classrooms, I battled against physical agony and navigated the treacherous waters of adolescence, all while cultivating a resilient spirit. Each whispered prayer, each tear shed in the solitude of my room, seemed to echo back to me, fortified and made manifest in unexpected blessings and bursts of inner strength.

The classrooms became arenas of both intellectual growth and inner struggle. The rustling of papers, the scratch of pencils on notebooks, and the sound of my own heartbeat as I faced another wave of pain converged into a symphony of determination. The whispered prayers and silent tears become rituals of strength and resilience, echoing through the halls of my soul.

Yet, amidst these trials, my high school days were not devoid of laughter, shared secrets, and the innocent wonder of first crushes. There were stolen glances and dreams of a beautiful future.

I would focus on a tree outside the classroom window. Sunlight filtered through the leaves, creating a dance of shadows on the ground. I could picture myself huddled underneath it, sharing secrets, prayers, and dreams, and for a brief moment, the pain and embarrassment would fade into the background, replaced by the warmth of friendship and youthful optimism.

Outside of school, my mother and I faced plenty of financial obstacles. I remember worrying often, yet she always had faith.

My mother, with her unwavering faith, practiced tithing —a testament to her devotion. "Give, and it shall be given unto you," she would say with conviction. I would watch her drop our very last coins into the collection basket at church, her belief steadfast that the Lord would provide. And somehow, He always did.

On days when our cupboards were bare and our spirits near broken, the divine would manifest in the most mundane of places: a forgotten bill in a jacket pocket, a misplaced bill turning up in her wallet—each discovery a small miracle, a reprieve in our ongoing battle with scarcity.

I can still see the quiet church, bathed in soft candlelight, as my mother placed those precious coins into the collection basket. The hushed reverence in the air, the sound of coins clinking, and the palpable faith that filled the room created a powerful atmosphere of devotion. The subsequent moments of unexpected blessings, like finding money in her pockets, were like rays of light breaking through the darkness, restoring hope and faith.

These moments left an indelible mark on my beliefs. I learned to see the hand of God in every aspect of my life—from the lady who allowed me to use her bathroom during one of my most vulnerable moments, though she turned me away thereafter, to the friends who would surround me when I would faint at school, oblivious to the pain that racked my body. Even as they unknowingly kept pace with my internal cries for relief, I saw them as angels in disguise, part of a grander scheme designed for my fortitude.

I often remember their kindness alike, their actions a testament to the goodness in the world. I can still feel the warmth of gratitude welling up within me as I recognize these acts of kindness as signs of divine providence.

I emerged from my high school years not unscarred but unbroken. My faith was no longer just a part of me but the core of me. The discipline of daily life without the convenience of modern amenities, the resilience learned in the face of chronic pain, and the joy found in the small, everyday miracles wove into the tapestry of my spirit a pattern of profound faith.

The day I stood at the threshold of graduation, looking back on the years of struggle and growth, the scars were there, but they were badges of honor. I saw them as reminders of the battles I'd fought and conquered. My faith, once a fragile seed, has grown into a mighty oak, its roots deep and unshakeable.

Every painful step, every moment of embarrassment, and every unexpected blessing shaped me into the woman I was becoming. It taught me that faith is not just about enduring but also about expecting the unexpected, finding grace in the midst of trials, and embracing the mysteries of a life touched by the divine hand of providence. My mother's mustard seed faith, which had grown into an avocado seed in her heart, had planted its roots deeply into mine, preparing me for a future filled with hope and the certainty that no matter the challenge, faith would carry me through.

PART II

BECOMING AN ADULT IN ASIA—MIRACLES AMIDST STRUGGLES

Faith sees the invisible, believes the unbelievable, and receives the impossible.

— CORRIE TEN BOOM

4

COLLEGE COMMUTE PERIL

In my journey through life, there was one unforgettable chapter that tested the very core of my faith. It was during my college years at Cebu Normal University in the Philippines where I pursued a Bachelor of Elementary Education. Those days were a whirlwind of challenges and triumphs, and one particular incident stands out like a beacon of divine intervention.

Each day, my college commute was a grueling adventure. The university was an hour from home, and I had to navigate the unpredictable traffic while changing public transportation multiple times. It was not a direct route; instead, I had to switch from one bus to another. The meager money I had was strictly reserved for transportation, leaving me with no funds for food.

But despite the hardships, my university days were filled with joy. I was grateful for the opportunity to study. This was a program my single mother could afford, and I passed the rigorous entrance exam of the Cebu Normal University, known for producing outstanding teachers. It was a state university with affordable tuition fees, and I also had a non-academic scholarship, which helped reduce my financial burden. To make ends meet, I worked as a part-time employee at the renowned fast-food chain Jollibee, which provided me with enough money to eat.

My daily routine was nothing short of grueling. It demanded unwavering determination and a relentless work ethic. Each day began at 4 am, as I roused myself from the embrace of sleep. The soft glow of dawn had yet to pierce the darkness outside my window. With bleary eyes and a heavy heart, I knew that another challenging day awaited me.

I allotted myself just one precious hour for a quick shower and breakfast. The chilling cold water I had to pump from the well offered a brief respite from the fatigue that clung to my bones. Breakfast was a simple affair, a meager reprieve from the demands of the day ahead. I needed to fortify myself for the trials that awaited.

By 5:30 am, I had to summon the strength to leave the comfort of my humble home. The early morning air was crisp, and the world was still cloaked in shadows. It was during these solitary moments that I offered my silent prayers, seeking divine guidance and protection for the arduous journey ahead.

Navigating the congested streets of the city was a daily battle. The rush-hour traffic was a relentless adversary, and every minute counted. My goal was to arrive at school by 7:30 am, a seemingly distant destination that required a Herculean effort to reach.

The hours at Cebu Normal University were grueling, filled with lectures, assignments, and the rigorous demands of academic life. I was pursuing a Bachelor of Elementary Education, a course that held the promise of a brighter future. But it came at a high cost, both in terms of financial strain and physical exhaustion.

After the last bell rang and the day's classes came to a close, my responsibilities were far from over. As part of my non-academic scholarship commitment, I was required to attend dance practice. These sessions were not mere extracurricular activities; they were essential for maintaining my scholarship. The dance floor became my sanctuary, a place where I could momentarily forget my fatigue and immerse myself in the rhythm and grace of movement.

The sun would have long dipped below the horizon by the time dance practice concluded, typically around 7:00 pm. I emerged from those sessions physically drained, my body aching and my stomach often gnawing with hunger. But there was no time for rest or nourishment. Duty called, and I had to answer.

Immediately after dance practice, I embarked on the next leg of my relentless journey. I made my way to my job at the fast-food restaurant. The closing shift was my domain, a grueling nighttime ordeal that often stretched until close to midnight. I juggled customer orders, worked tirelessly to maintain the restaurant's cleanliness, and ensured that every detail was cared for.

When my shift finally came to an end, I was physically and mentally drained. But there was no respite awaiting me. The clock ticked relentlessly, and I knew I had to catch the hour-long bus ride back home. The bus was my conduit between the world of work and the embrace of sleep, and I clung to it like a lifeline.

I hoped to steal a few precious hours of rest before the cycle began anew. The hour of midnight often came and went before I could close my eyes, and sleep was a brief oasis in the desert of my exhausting routine.

This daily grind was my reality, a relentless cycle of work and study that tested the limits of my endurance. But through it all, I held onto my dreams and unwavering faith. It was the driving force that propelled me forward, the source of strength that enabled me to persevere in the face of adversity.

One of the stark realities of my life at that time was the absence of a cell phone. Eventually, a neighbor sold us one at a reduced price, and my mother made installment payments to ensure I had a means of communication. However, I was the only one in the family with a phone, and I had to use it sparingly, usually relying on my cousin or aunt to convey messages to my mother.

Amid the chaos of my university and work commitments, I also took on a side job teaching cheer dance to another school. They were preparing for a competition, and a friend had recommended me as a coach. It was a fantastic opportunity, but it meant additional late-night practices in unfamiliar parts of the city.

One particular night, I finished practice well past midnight, and as I ventured home along an unfamiliar route, fear began to creep in. The darkness held uncertainty, and I was keenly aware of the dangerous reputation of that area. Night after night, it was plagued by robberies, gun violence, and pickpocketing incidents.

The air inside the bus was thick with tension, and an uneasy feeling settled in my gut. It was a sensation that transcended the ordinary discomfort one might feel during a late-night commute. The darkness outside seemed to encroach upon the bus, and the shadows that danced on the fringes of my vision took on a menacing quality. It was as if the night itself conspired to heighten my unease.

As I clutched my bag closer to my chest, my heart began to race, its thunderous beats reverberating in my ears. Every instinct in my body screamed danger, and a chilling sense of foreboding washed over me. It was in that moment that I noticed him—a man with red eyes, his face obscured by the gloom of the bus's interior, a cigarette dangling carelessly from his lips.

His demeanor was unsettling, his movements sluggish and unsteady, as though he teetered on the precipice of intoxication. The pungent scent of alcohol hung heavy in the air around him. He took a seat beside me, and my heart leaped into my throat, rendering me immobile. Paralyzed by fear, I didn't dare to move a muscle, not even to draw a breath.

In the pit of my stomach, I felt an instinctual understanding that this man harbored sinister intentions. It was as though an invisible shroud of malevolence enveloped him, and I knew my safety was in peril. Panic surged through my veins, and I silently implored for a way out of this nightmarish situation.

In that terrifying moment, with the threat of harm looming over me like a dark cloud, I turned to the only source of solace and strength I had always known: My unwavering faith in God. With every ounce of conviction, I prayed fervently for protection, my silent words a desperate plea for divine intervention to rescue me from this perilous abyss.

The seconds felt like an eternity, each passing moment an agonizing test of my resolve. And then, in a miraculous twist of fate, the bus screeched to a sudden, jolting halt. The abruptness of the stop sent a collective gasp rippling through the passengers, and I could hardly believe my senses.

To my astonishment, the bus doors swung open, and a couple boarded. It was a young woman, one of the students I had been coaching in cheer dance, accompanied by her boyfriend. As they entered, their eyes scanned the dimly lit bus, and it was as if fate had guided their gaze directly to me.

In an instant, they recognized the dire situation I was in. Without a moment's hesitation, they gestured for me to join them. It was a lifeline extended in the midst of a storm; an act of kindness born from their instinctive understanding of the danger I faced.

Sensing the protective presence of these strangers, the man with sinister intentions hastily retreated from the bus. As he stepped off into the darkness of the night, a collective sigh of relief rippled through the bus. The threat had dissipated, and I was safe once more.

It was a moment that defied explanation, a testament to the power of faith and the mysterious workings of divine intervention. In the face of imminent danger, my unwavering belief in God had served as my anchor, guiding me through the darkest moments. And when I had cried out for help, it felt as though the heavens themselves had responded, sending these two kind-hearted individuals to stand as guardians in my hour of need.

This harrowing encounter left an indelible mark on my heart, a reminder of the miraculous ways in which faith can illuminate the darkest of paths and guide us to safety when all hope seems lost.

It was a moment of sheer relief, and tears welled up in my eyes. I knew, without a shadow of a doubt, that I had been saved by grace, that divine protection had intervened to keep me safe. What I didn't know at the time was that this man had a reputation for robbing passengers on buses during the night, and he had a knife in his pocket that night.

As I reflected on that harrowing experience, I couldn't help but marvel at the incredible timing of the couple's unexpected presence on that bus. They weren't supposed to be there; their car had suffered an engine failure, and they had patiently waited for an empty bus to come along. At that moment, I saw God's hand at work, orchestrating events to protect and save me from harm.

This was just one of the many times I felt God had sent an angel to watch over me. I believe that my mother's prayers played a key role in keeping me safe. With only the two of us in this world, I was still young and vulnerable, and her heartfelt pleas to God on my behalf were a source of strength and comfort.

My faith in God was my refuge during this perilous commute and a growing anchor in my life. It was during these dangerous times that my faith deepened and solidified. I learned to rely on God's guidance and protection, trusting He would always be there to help me navigate the storms of life.

He saved me again that night, as He had done countless times before. My journey was a testament to the power of unwavering faith, divine intervention, and the resilience of the human spirit. In my darkest hours, I had discovered that my faith could withstand the fiercest storms, just like an unshakeable mighty oak.

5

THE HARROWING DOG ATTACK

It had been a time of transition in my life. I had recently graduated from college, a significant milestone that opened up new possibilities for my future. But along with that achievement came the reality of financial constraints. My mother and I, always a team in the face of adversity, had once again found ourselves on the hunt for a more affordable place to live.

We moved to a rental room further away from the city, a decision driven by the need to cut costs and make ends meet. This new room was nestled in a quiet neighborhood, but it was far from the bustling urban streets I was accustomed to while going to school. It was a place where the city lights no longer reached, and the nights were enveloped in profound darkness, illuminated only by the faint glow of the stars and the distant chirping of crickets.

To support our modest life in this unfamiliar territory, I took up tutoring jobs, going to students' homes late into the night to help them with their studies. It was a source of income that had become essential for our survival, but it also meant that I had to travel the long, unlit pathway back home in the darkness, far from the comfort of street-lights and the buzz of the city.

The night in question was one of those dark, moonless nights when the air was thick with the sounds of nature. The pathway I walked was devoid of any guiding lights, shrouded in an eerie silence broken only by the occasional rustling of leaves and the distant calls of nocturnal creatures. I could feel the weight of responsibility on my shoulders, knowing that my mother was waiting for me at home and my income was vital for our livelihood.

With each step, I was aware of the isolation around me, and my senses were heightened by the darkness. Despite the fear that crept into my thoughts, I remained determined to reach our home safely.

Little did I know that this seemingly routine journey would become a pivotal moment in my life, a moment when the strength of my faith and resilience would be put to the ultimate test. The unexpected encounter with evil would not only challenge my physical well-being but also serve as a profound lesson in the unwavering power of belief in the face of adversity.

As I reached the entrance of the property, I suddenly realized that the gate was locked. Panic started to set in. I had no idea that the pathway was privately owned and that they would close it at 10 pm. I felt like a prisoner, trapped in the darkness with no way to reach the safety of my home.

I screamed for my mother, my voice trembling with fear. It was then that I felt an eerie sensation crawl over my body. Out of nowhere, a pack of dogs appeared outside the gate, howling and barking ferociously. They were foaming at the mouth, showing their teeth, and I knew I was in grave danger.

I screamed louder, desperately calling out for my mother to hear me and open the gate. I stood frozen, screaming for what felt like an eternity. The pack of dogs seemed relentless, and I had no idea where they were all coming from. I was trapped, unable to turn back to the road, which was a long, dark walk with no streetlights–a path filled with unexpected dangers.

Desperately, I began to repeat the verses of Psalm 23, a prayer of protection that my mother had taught me since I was young. It was the same prayer I had used when I had nightmares as a child, when I was lost in the woods, or when I felt alone on that city bus. It was a prayer that had always brought me comfort, and now, in the face of this terrifying ordeal, it became my lifeline (King James, n.d.):

> *The LORD is my shepherd; I shall not want.*
> *He maketh me to lie down in green pastures: he*
>   *leadeth me beside the still waters.*
> *He restoreth my soul: he leadeth me in the paths*
>   *of righteousness for his name's sake.*
> *Yea, though I walk through the valley of the*
>   *shadow of death, I will fear no evil: for thou*
>   *art with me; thy rod and thy staff they*
>   *comfort me.*
> *Thou preparest a table before me in the presence*
>   *of mine enemies: thou anointest my head*
>   *with oil; my cup runneth over.*
> *Surely goodness and mercy shall follow me all the*
>   *days of my life: and I will dwell in the house*
>   *of the LORD forever.*

Psalm 23 is a comforting and reassuring passage that speaks of God's care, guidance, and protection, often symbolized by the image of a shepherd caring for his flock. I have always found solace in it, repeating it in times of trouble or when seeking spiritual comfort and strength.

In that moment of sheer terror, I cried, yelled, and prayed to the Lord to save me. Even though I was inside the locked gate, it was a corrugated one with a big square hole in it, and their mouths could still fit through, dripping with saliva.

As I continued to scream for help, the gatekeeper of the property was awakened by an alarm he had set. My mother had informed him what time I would be coming home, so he had set this alarm to let me in. As he staggered outside to find me frantic, he was confused. Out of breath, tears streaming down my face, I tried to gather myself to tell everyone what was happening. Strangely, he had not heard the dog howls, nor had the neighbors or my mother. And then, I looked around. Their faces look back at me. As suddenly as the dogs had appeared, they were gone. The air was now filled with silence, completely quiet. It was as if they had vanished into thin air.

I was not hallucinating or dreaming; I was utterly terrified. My body was covered in goosebumps, and I felt a strange, airy sensation blowing on the nape of my neck. I knew that I had been on the brink of a life-threatening situation.

In the aftermath of the dog attack, I couldn't help but reflect on everything that had happened. Hadn't I believed in the verses my mother had taught me? Hadn't I held onto my faith and the songs of Jesus that had always made me feel calm, even when it seemed like the devil himself was attacking me, not just physically but mentally as well?

As I thought back on the terrifying events of that fateful night, a chilling revelation washed over me, leaving an indelible mark on my soul. It was an eerie and unsettling realization that the previous tenant of the place we had rented had experienced a deeply tragic fate. This tenant, who had inhabited the very space we now called home, had kept five imposing dogs as his companions and, heartbreakingly, had chosen to end his own life.

The details of his final moments were haunting. The neighbors had recounted hearing him yell at someone in the darkness, but soon after, he was left in eerie solitude. It was as though a shroud of darkness had descended upon him, leaving him alone with his demons, both literal and figurative. The circumstances surrounding his untimely death left an ominous cloud of unanswered questions hanging over our new room.

Our rental room was situated beside an old caimito tree, its gnarled branches casting eerie shadows in the moonlight. The tree, with its mystical presence, had garnered a reputation among the locals as a place of otherworldly occurrences. Rumors had circulated that an evil spirit roamed the vicinity at night, an unseen malevolent force that seemed to manifest itself in inexplicable ways. The mere thought of such supernatural occurrences sent shivers down our spines, and it was impossible to ignore the foreboding atmosphere that enveloped our surroundings.

But it was in the face of this ominous backdrop that I came to fully comprehend the immense power of faith and the unwavering belief in God. It was faith that had served as my shield that night when the pack of dogs had closed in, their menacing presence threatening to consume me. It was faith that had provided me with the strength to call upon the verses of Psalm 23, seeking divine protection in a moment of dire need.

My faith was more than a mere refuge; it was a steadfast anchor in the tempest of adversity. It was a testament to the resilience that resides within us when we hold fast to our beliefs. The harrowing experience of that dog attack illuminated the profound truth that, even in the darkest of moments, our unwavering faith can be the guiding light that leads us toward growth, cultural understanding, healing, and the unwavering strength to overcome life's most formidable challenges. It was a lesson etched into the fabric of my being, a lesson that would continue to shape my journey in the chapters yet to be written.

FROM TORN RESUME TO TRIUMPH

After we left the house we rented in the countryside, we moved back to the city once again. I was 22 years old and had been working for Cebu Pacific Airlines for four years. It was a bittersweet transition, leaving behind the rural tranquility that had both its moments of beauty and harrowing experiences, like the dog attack I endured. Life in the countryside was far from easy, with its rugged terrain, lack of public transportation, and the constant need to rely on natural resources. But as we settled back into the city, I couldn't help but feel a sense of relief. The city was where I felt more comfortable despite its own set of challenges.

My mother and I rented a small room near the airport because it was close to our workplaces. Our daily existence was marked by the struggle to make ends meet. I juggled work, responsibilities, and dreams, all while trying to provide for my little family. Little did I know that this period of my life, marked by financial hardships in a third-world country, would lead me to a remarkable journey of faith, resilience, and unexpected opportunities.

When you work for an airline like I did, you would get great discounts on flights, especially domestic ones. For this reason, I never thought twice when I would notice colleagues traveling to the city. I just assumed they were visiting friends or family. One day, they insisted that I come along. I had thought it would be nice to spend the day away just visiting the sites and relaxing. I had no idea what was in store. Once on the plan, I finally clued in. My colleagues had actually been traveling to the city to apply for jobs with larger airlines abroad. As they sat in their seats, reviewing their polished resumes and practicing their interview skills, I felt this sinking feeling in my stomach. What was I going to do? I wasn't at all prepared for this. I also felt this twinge of excitement at the opportunities that might unfold for me with this type of job.

I knew that the only resume I had available to me was sitting in my email. I hastily retrieved it and started to update it. Once we landed, I had mere moments to quickly print three copies. I also photocopied my photo identification. I expected to give my resume to two of the major airlines in the Middle East—Emirates Airlines and Qatar Airways. The resumes I handed to them were perfect, neatly presented with every detail in place. The next moments were a whirlwind of handing over resumes, smiling, and asking questions.

Then, something unexpected happened. One of my friends told me about another airline in the Middle East that was hiring. We rushed to their hiring booth, and I tried to pass my resume. That's when I realized the shocking truth—my resume was torn because I had mistakenly stuck my identification picture onto another page in my hurry. I looked down at the stack of pristine and flawless resumes, and there lay mine, torn and seemingly insignificant among the rest, looking like discarded trash.

If I am being honest, I didn't have high hopes for that application. It was dirty, it was torn, and it stood out for all the wrong reasons. I felt okay with this because I didn't even know which country in the Middle East this airline was based. I had no clue where I would end up working.

Can you imagine my shock when I received a phone call from the airline for an interview? I couldn't believe it. I thought it might be a scam or a mistake. After all, I was the one who had handed them a torn and dirty resume. I spent some time trying to research this company, and I wasn't coming up with a lot of information. They were located in a remote part of the Middle East, Oman, so no, this wouldn't be considered a popular airline.

The other major airlines also called me for interviews, but I didn't like the terms of their contracts. It was "Omanair" that offered me the benefits I desired and a better overall package than the others, which was completely unex-pected. Not many people had applied there because it wasn't as famous as Dubai or Qatar, and that raised some concerns.

I continued to research Oman, as it was a place I knew very little about. There weren't many resources available, and I was anxious about what to expect. I prayed for God to guide me in the right direction and headed for that interview.

The day of the interview was a pivotal moment in my life, and I remember it like it was yesterday. The night before had been restless, plagued by nerves that kept me tossing and turning in my modest room near the airport. Thoughts raced through my mind: Would I be good enough? Was this torn resume a glaring mistake that would cost me the opportunity of a lifetime? But there was no turning back now.

Determined to face the day head-on, I rose early, long before the first rays of sunlight painted the city's skyline. The room was dimly lit, and the air was thick with anticipation. I knew that a hearty breakfast was essential to fuel both my body and my spirit for the challenges that lay ahead. With trembling hands, I prepared a simple yet satisfying meal, the comforting aroma of freshly brewed coffee filling the room.

As I savored each bite, my mind raced with a mixture of excitement and anxiety. I couldn't afford to be late, not on a day that held the promise of changing my life forever. With a final sip of coffee, I donned my best attire, a suit that was meticulously pressed and chosen with great care. It was a symbol of the professionalism I aimed to convey.

The interview location loomed ahead, a nondescript building that held the key to my future. Arriving well in advance, I felt a sense of calm wash over me as I gazed at the unfamiliar surroundings. The early morning sun cast a warm glow, a hopeful omen that seemed to say, "You're exactly where you're meant to be."

The process that followed was nothing short of miraculous. I was the first one to be interviewed, a stroke of fortune that I couldn't have predicted. Sitting in that room, I felt a mixture of anticipation and gratitude, my torn resume resting on the table in front of me as a tangible reminder of the journey that had brought me here.

The interview itself went surprisingly smoothly. I answered questions with confidence, my passion for aviation and unwavering belief in my abilities shining through. When the interview concluded, I was offered the job on the spot, a moment of pure astonishment that left me momentarily speechless.

As I left the interview room, I couldn't help but look back at the torn, seemingly insignificant resume that had been my ticket to this life-changing opportunity. It was a symbol of the unexpected twists and turns that life could take and a testament to the power of faith. That resume, which I had thought might hinder me, had instead opened doors I had never imagined.

I had once dreamt of working in the glitzy cities of Doha or Dubai with renowned airlines like Emirates, envisioning a life of luxury and prestige. But God had a different plan for me, one that unfolded in a way I could never have foreseen. He had orchestrated this remarkable turn of events, guiding my steps and leading me down a path I hadn't dared to imagine.

Throughout this journey, I found myself constantly calling upon my faith. My mother's reminders to pray anywhere, anytime, and everywhere echoed in my heart. Despite my preferences and desires, I prayed for guidance, trusting that God knew what was best for me, even when I had doubts. I had once been naive enough to imagine myself living in a tent and riding camels, but I had learned that God's plans were far more intricate and purposeful.

My faith remained unshakeable, a steadfast anchor in the midst of uncertainty. I often found myself throwing my hands in the air, proclaiming, "I will do my best, and God will do the rest!" It was a mantra that had carried me through life's trials and tribulations, a reminder that I was not alone on this journey.

This chapter of my life served as a powerful testament to the transformative power of faith and divine intervention. It was a reminder that our plans and preferences may not always align with God's purpose for us. Yet, when we let go of our own expectations and trust in His plan, even a torn resume can lead to triumph. It was a humbling experience that strengthened my faith and taught me to recognize the miracles that can unfold in everyday life, reminding me that with faith, resilience, and unwavering belief, we can overcome even the most daunting of challenges.

PART III

CHALLENGES IN THE MIDDLE EAST—FAITH UNDER FIRE

Overcoming obstacles starts with a positive attitude and faith that God will see you through.

— ANONYMOUS

7

THE BATTLE AGAINST THE BULLIES

Bullying had been a relentless and unwelcome companion on the journey of my life, casting a long, daunting shadow that refused to dissipate. Its roots dug deep into the soil of my earliest memories, creating a dark and oppressive cloud that hung over what should have been a bright and hopeful existence.

Growing up, I was raised by my remarkable single mother in the rugged and picturesque landscapes of one of the mountainous islands of the Philippines. It was just the two of us— an only child and a determined mother—navigating a world where resources were as scarce as opportunities were few and far between.

From the very beginning, the odds seemed stacked against me. As a child raised in a single-parent household, I was an anomaly in a society that often placed a heavy emphasis on traditional family structures. It was a society where the presence of a father was seen as a measure of one's worth, and the absence of one became a glaring mark of distinction.

The early chapters of my life were marked by financial hardships and a relentless struggle to make ends meet in a third-world country. Yet, amidst the challenges that seemed insurmountable, one thing remained constant— our unshakable dream of education and our faith.

As I grew older, the specter of bullying cast its shadow not only in my family life but also in the wider world. The scars from my childhood bullying experiences ran deep, shaping my self-esteem and influencing the way I approached relationships. It was a torment that extended far beyond the confines of my home, following me into school, college, and the workplace.

This chapter of my life is a testament to the enduring struggle against the bullies who crossed my path, from those early childhood tormentors to the college dance club members who questioned my place among them. It chronicles the battles waged against workplace adversaries who sought to undermine my confidence and the challenges of forging a life in a foreign land, where cultural differences only exacerbated my sense of isolation.

Yet, through it all, there was a guiding light, an unwavering faith that helped me navigate the darkest of tunnels. This part of my story is a testament to the transformative power of faith, an exploration of how it became the cornerstone of my resilience, hope, and healing in the face of adversity. It's a journey of growth, cultural struggle, loss, healing, resilience, and faith—a journey that I am eager to share in the hope that it may inspire and uplift others facing their own battles against the bullies of life.

EARLY CHILDHOOD BULLYING

My struggle with bullying began when I was just five years old, an innocent child who had yet to comprehend the complexities of the world around me. It was a time when the innocence of childhood should have prevailed, and life's burdens should have been far from my young shoulders. However, fate had other plans, and it was my very own cousins who first introduced me to the cruel reality of bullying. Their actions and words cut deep, leaving wounds that would take years to heal.

Our days were filled with adventures in the breathtaking beauty of the natural world that surrounded us. We ran through fields of tall grass, climbed trees that seemed to touch the sky, and waded in crystal-clear streams that meandered through our lush, mountainous home. These were the moments when life should have been carefree, and the bonds of family should have grown stronger. Yet, for me, it was a time when every victory, every moment of joy, was overshadowed by taunts and jeers.

My cousins, those I expected to be my playmates and allies, were the first to turn against me. As we engaged in our childish games, their words were like arrows aimed at my heart. They would mockingly say that it was acceptable if I won because, in their eyes, they were the fortunate ones with fathers in their lives. Their snickers and cruel remarks pierced through the laughter and camaraderie of our play, leaving me feeling isolated and dejected.

I would often hear their hurtful remarks echoing in my ears, "Who cares if you won? At least we have a father." It was as though my status as a child from a single mother marked me as inferior, an object of pity and ridicule in their eyes. They had been told by their family to take pity on me, and they followed that directive with a relentless cruelty that defied my understanding.

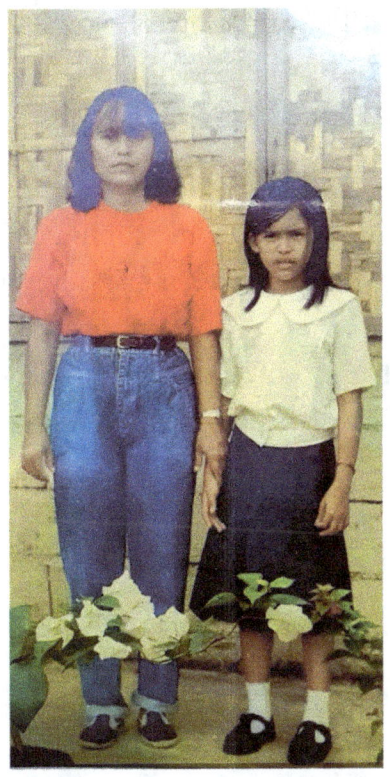

These early experiences with bullying left an indelible mark on my psyche. They shattered my innocence and instilled a sense of unworthiness that would plague me for years to come. The wounds may not have been physical, but they ran deep, affecting my self-esteem and leaving me with a lingering sense of inadequacy.

It was in the midst of these turbulent childhood years that I began to grasp the harsh realities of the world, where the absence of a father figure became a source of scorn rather than compassion. The bullying I endured from my cousins was just the beginning of a long and tumultuous journey, one that would continue to shape my self-perception and influence the way I approached relationships and adversity in the years to come.

As I went to school, the bullying continued. It was as if my lack of a father figure marked me as different, as someone to be looked down upon. It weighed heavily on my self-esteem, and it had a profound impact on my social life and relationships. I struggled to make friends, to fit in, and to feel like I belonged anywhere. The scars of those early experiences would linger, shaping my self-perception and leaving me vulnerable to future bullies.

BULLYING AMONG ROOMMATES

College brought with it new challenges and a fresh wave of bullying. You see, I grew up without money, without the latest fashion or new things. Food and shelter were always our priority. I was just a simple girl with humble means, lacking the expensive possessions and fashionable attire that seemed to define worth in the eyes of my peers. To make matters worse, I was accepted into college on a dance scholarship. This lowered my tuition greatly. The problem with this was that this was a realm dominated by those who were wealthy. I didn't belong there, or so they thought. They couldn't understand why I, a girl without the latest gadgets and designer clothes, had the audacity to be a part of their world.

During dance practice, I faced the relentless cruelty of my fellow club members. They teased me, insulted me, and made me feel like an outsider. One of the lead dancers, in particular, took pleasure in publicly humiliating me, labeling me as stupid because I couldn't keep up with the choreography. What she didn't know was that I had no time to rest after practice. I would head straight to my job at a fast-food chain, working late into the night just to make ends meet. I did this every single day, running on just a few hours of sleep. I was exhausted, not stupid.

But I clung to my dream of education, knowing that dancing helped keep my tuition fees low. I endured the bullying, praying to God for the strength to remain resilient in the face of adversity.

WORKPLACE BULLYING

As an adult working in the airline industry in Cebu, I encountered yet another form of bullying. My manager seemed to harbor a deep hatred for me. No matter what I did, she always found something negative to say. I was the girl from the mountains, the "poor" girl wearing clothes that were far from fashionable. To her, I was an easy target for her cruel remarks and belittling behavior.

The workplace should have been a place of growth and opportunity, but instead, it became a battleground for my self-esteem and well-being. The constant barrage of negativity left me questioning my abilities and my worth.

Amid all these trials and tribulations, my unwavering faith in God became my refuge. It was the one constant in my life, a source of strength and resilience that I could always turn to. My faith was my light in the darkest of times, my anchor when I felt adrift in a sea of adversity.

I remembered the lessons my mother had taught me about dealing with bullies: "Leave them alone. Don't fight back. Don't stoop to their level." It was a mantra born of our financial struggles and the absence of a father to protect me. While it was difficult to follow this advice, I held onto it, believing that it was the right path.

I cried alone in the bathroom or confided in my mother about the torment I endured. She offered one simple but powerful solution: "Pray for them." It was a concept I clung to, praying fervently each night, seeking strength from a higher power to carry me through the storms of life.

Life took me to the Middle East, to a foreign land with a vastly different culture from my own. I found myself often looked down upon by my colleagues from the big city. They came from wealth and privilege, and their prejudice was evident.

The bullying continued, and I felt like an outsider once again. It was bewildering to see how some people could be triggered by my mere presence. Perhaps they saw me as just an island girl, someone lesser than them. The lessons I had learned from my mother echoed in my mind, and I hesitated to fight back. Instead, I chose to leave those who bullied me and sought refuge with a kind-hearted barista named Mendy, who allowed me to stay at her place in exchange for rent. This allowed me to no longer have to live with those I worked with and endure the daily bullying.

I believed deep in my heart that God had guided me to this place and would provide me with the strength to face these bullies. I knew that my mother prayed fervently for my safety and that faith in God was the thread that held me together.

The transformative power of faith became evident as I navigated the minefield of bullies throughout my life. It wasn't about revenge or retaliation; it was about finding the strength within myself to rise above the cruelty of others. It was about holding onto hope when darkness threatened to consume me. It was about healing the wounds that had been inflicted on my self-esteem and soul.

In the midst of adversity, faith was my rock. It was the unwavering belief that God had a purpose for me, that He saw my struggles, and that He would never abandon me. It was the understanding that even in the face of bullies, I was not alone. My faith gave me the resilience to keep going, to keep believing in myself, and to keep striving for a better future.

So, as I faced the bullies in my life, whether they were childhood tormentors, college dance peers, workplace adversaries, or colleagues in a foreign land, I clung to my faith. I prayed for them, not out of weakness, but out of strength. I forgave them, not because they deserved it, but because I deserved peace. And in doing so, I found the healing and transformation that had eluded me for so long.

The battle against the bullies was a long and arduous one, but it was a battle I could face with unwavering faith in my heart. It was a battle that ultimately shaped me into the resilient, hopeful, and empowered person I am today.

8

CONFRONTING THE ASSAULTS
AND TRAUMA

At that moment, as a young 24-year-old woman living in Oman, I found myself in a situation I could have never anticipated when I left my home in the Philippines. Life had taken me far from the familiar mountains of my childhood, and I had become the sole breadwinner for my family. Gone were the days when I was surrounded by the comforting presence of my mother and extended family; instead, I had chosen to move in with a friend in this foreign land, a decision born out of a desire for independence and a yearning to forge my own path.

Living in Oman was a stark departure from what I had known. The Middle Eastern culture, with its unique languages, customs, and traditions, was both captivating and bewildering. Every day was a challenge as I navigated the unfamiliar terrain, trying to adapt and fit into a world so different from my own. My job as a ground crew brought with it a mix of excitement and adversity as I jetted across borders, but little did I know that I would soon confront a series of traumatic events that would push the limits of my faith and resilience.

The airline I worked for provided us with an allowance instead of transportation, which meant I had to rely on taxis to commute to and from work. Living alone in this foreign land, I often found myself alone in these taxis, which was not an unusual occurrence. In fact, I often felt safer when the taxi was full, surrounded by other passengers.

However, one fateful night, I found myself alone in the taxi, and the driver, a young Arab man, began to cross boundaries that should never be crossed. His hands wandered inappropriately, and he seemed to believe that he had the right to touch my body without my consent. In his mind, my body belonged to him, and I had no rights. Fear gripped me, and I had to resort to self-defense, punching his arm and pulling his hair in a desperate attempt to make him stop. But he was undeterred by my actions, continuing to violate my personal space. I gave thought to smashing his face with my heavy work bag, but a wave came over me, making me question whether my life was worth it.

In sheer terror, I screamed at him to halt the taxi, my voice cracking with fear and anguish. Eventually, he complied, and as soon as the vehicle came to a stop, I bolted from the cab, my heart pounding in my chest. Tears streamed down my face as I fled from the scene, leaving behind a traumatic experience that would haunt me for a long time to come.

Another incident, eerily similar, occurred a year later. Once again, I would find myself in a taxi, but I was at ease knowing others were in there with me. Then, the taxi would stop, and they would pile out, leaving me, yet again, alone. I immediately sensed danger as the driver's behavior grew increasingly odd. He would drive past those waiting on the street for a ride. He was increasing his speed and driving recklessly. Then, he became inappropriate. I would look over to see him unbuttoning his pants and removing his penis. Right there, inside of the taxi where I felt trapped, he began to pleasure himself while driving. More than once, he would grab my hand in an attempt to place it on his private parts. I was frozen in fear. I calmly told him that I would smash the window if he didn't stop the car immediately. He pulled over after finishing pleasuring himself and let me out in the middle of nowhere. I would now have to find my way home, sobbing and shaking while other taxis would pass, honking and yelling horrid things.

Another time, I was simply walking home from the grocery store. It was my day off, and I had a long list of errands to get done. My arms were full, carrying bags of groceries. Out of nowhere, I got chills and a sense of danger over my body. A man came up from behind and started groping me. I was shocked and violated. I screamed, threatening to call the police, but he just snickered at me, telling me to "Go ahead." I felt powerless, carrying the weight of these traumatic experiences, but I couldn't let them break me.

Then came the most devastating blow. I was on the night shift, and my fiancé was out of town. We had recently had a huge fight because I had caught him cheating. We agreed to work on things.

That night I was scheduled to start work at 9 pm. I had found a friendly and reliable transport service driver who would usually take me to work, but he forgot to pick me up, leaving me to walk alone in the dark. I had to walk about ten minutes to reach the city and find another taxi. As I walked, I felt a presence behind me, and suddenly, a man grabbed me and covered my mouth. He dragged me toward a dark alley, but I managed to break free and hide in the shadows. As I hid, I reached for my phone, and in desperation, the number I called was that of my fiancé's business. My voice shaking, I asked to speak to him, and they informed me that he was out of the country visiting his girlfriend.

My heart was shattered, and I felt utterly betrayed. I had endured so much already, and now this. I picked myself up out of the shadows and made my way to work. I still don't know how I managed. I continued to work that night, but my trauma weighed heavily on me. I kept going to the bathroom to hide my tears, feeling like I was unraveling. I had been attacked and violated by a stranger and my fiancé ... again.

As if all this wasn't enough for one person to handle, my fiancé decided to try and ruin my life. You see, the truth was all coming out. He had been fired from his job, and his "girlfriend" broke it off with him. This meant he had no money and no place to go. He didn't know I had this information about him. He knew the easy solution was to win me back, and when that wasn't successful, he took it to a whole new level. You see, he was a white man in a country where that meant power over women. He went to the police station and told them I had purposely broken his property. That I was evil, that I had cheated on him and was now trying to ruin his life. He had a friend at the police station draw up a subpoena telling me I had to appear in an Arabian court. Police were constantly banging on my door, asking questions. Worse than that, I had someone I considered a friend sneaking my ex into my flat. I arrived home to find him there, and he locked us together in my bathroom, claiming we were a "Romeo and Juliet" love story. I was honestly afraid I would die in that bathroom. I just kept my eyes on the floor, my arms wrapped around myself for protection, and praying to God.

I would end up getting an order of protection so he could no longer come near me, and if he did, he would have to go to jail.

With all that I had endured, my body and mind were in a constant state of trauma. I only slept in two-hour intervals. I couldn't eat. I worked every possible overtime shift I could because I never felt safe outside or in my home.

In the midst of these traumatic experiences, I had lost my faith. Where was he in all of these times of pain and suffering? Why was it necessary I travel this path? It felt like God had forsaken me. I watched as my coworkers lived their lives. They seemed to float through things without issue while I felt trapped in a never-ending cycle of pain and fear. I was alone, and I didn't feel that protection and love I had always felt from God.

But as I lay in bed one night, I realized that even in my darkest moments, God had been with me. Despite the betrayals and the horrors, I had faced, I had survived. The police incident with my ex-fiancé had a silver lining—he was no longer allowed near me, and I could finally break free from his toxic grip. I had been trapped in a cycle of abuse with this man for quite some time. Allowing him to treat me less than I deserved. When I was able to calm down and reflect back on the devastating traumas I went through, God was there to protect me. I could have died. I am alive, and I am stronger.

I had every reason to be angry, but I also had reasons to be thankful. I had learned to rely on my faith to find strength in the face of adversity. Even when I felt abandoned, I knew that I wasn't alone. I may have lost my faith temporarily, but I would find my way back to it, stronger and more resilient than ever.

9

UNEXPECTED ANGELS—THE HOSPITAL AND THE STRANGERS

A s I sit here and reflect upon the events of this chapter, my heart swells with gratitude and amazement at the remarkable way in which divine intervention and unexpected angels touched my life during my time in Oman. At the age of 29, I was still a long way from my homeland in the Philippines, toiling tirelessly in the Middle East to provide for my mother. Little did I know that these experiences would become pivotal chapters in my life story as well. They would help restore my faith in God.

It all began on a seemingly ordinary night—the night of my dear friend's birthday celebration. I had never been one to indulge in alcohol, but on this particular evening, I decided to partake in a single sip of red wine to accompany a delectable fish dinner. It appeared harmless at first, but within moments, my world began to unravel. My vision blurred and distorted, and nausea overtook me like a relentless tide. Panic set in as I found myself uncontrollably vomiting, and to my utter horror, the contents were a ghastly shade of green. Weakness washed over me, and the room spun around like a grotesque carnival ride. In the throes of this terrifying experience, I made a solemn vow never to let alcohol pass my lips again.

As the hours wore on, my condition took a harrowing nosedive. I could no longer stand, and the agony in my abdomen was beyond description. Each time I made an attempt to move my body at all, the pain would overcome me. My friend, alarmed by my deteriorating state, made the urgent call for an ambulance. Inside that ambulance, I felt suspended between the realms of life and death, each bump in the road sending shockwaves of torment through my body. With every jolt, I beseeched the driver to proceed with the utmost caution.

Finally, we arrived at the bustling emergency department of a public Arabian hospital. The atmosphere was overwhelming, and I was a solitary figure, far from the comfort of my homeland. The medical personnel bombarded me with questions and subjected me to a battery of tests. It seemed I was getting nowhere, no scans of my abdomen, just question after question. Fear gnawed at my heart as I awaited answers, alone and vulnerable in a foreign land. To complicate matters, they detected traces of alcohol in my bloodstream—an issue of grave consequence in a culture where drinking was viewed as a sin.

Despite the excruciating pain and mounting anxiety, I languished in that hospital, with seemingly endless hours slipping by without any medical attention.

My friends eventually tracked me down in the hospital. Once the staff realized I worked for the airline, they began to show more interest in my case, driven perhaps by the hope of securing discounts on airline tickets. Even so, it took an agonizingly long time before they conducted an X-ray of my stomach, and the results proved inconclusive. To err on the side of caution, they administered a potent cocktail of painkillers and sent me on my way.

The following day, I resumed my duties at work, still under the influence of prescribed medication for pain. Little did I know that the ordeal was far from over. A sudden allergic reaction sent me rushing to the airport clinic for treatment. It was then that I realized the Arabian hospital had inadvertently caused more harm than good.

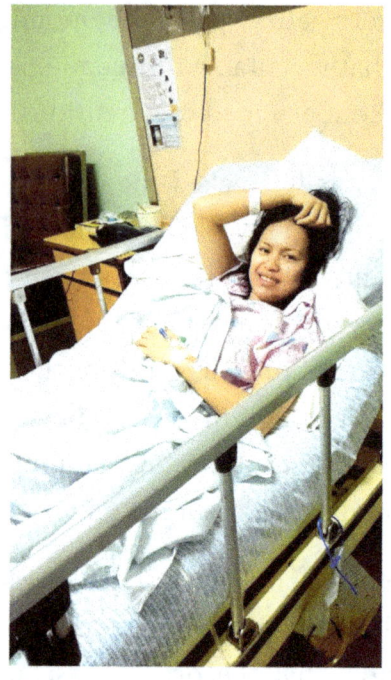

A month later, still in a tremendous amount of pain, I seized the opportunity to take a leave of absence and journeyed back to the Philippines. There, I sought the counsel of my OBGYN, who promptly dispatched me to the emergency room. Through a careful series of inquiries, she unraveled the mystery: a ruptured ovarian cyst. Miraculously, my robust immune system had shielded me from the dire consequences of this condition. Life-saving surgery was performed to cleanse my uterine wall, and I emerged from that experience with a renewed appreciation for the fragility of life.

Yet loneliness enveloped me in that hospital room once again. My mom had left to get me some clothes but spent hours traveling to her home and feeding her pets. The same feeling of dark isolation consumed me yet again. I sought refuge in conversation with God, even though the reasons behind these trials remained elusive.

Fast-forward to my 31st year, still living and working in Oman. One fateful day, I was in a hurry when an unforeseen catastrophe struck. I was rushing and stepped awkwardly onto some small stairs. I then found myself unable to step on my left foot. The pain was excruciating, and I had no choice but to drag my limp leg. At first, I assumed it was a minor vein issue. However, as my leg began to swell, I realized I needed urgent medical attention. The orthopedic doctor's diagnosis was devastating— a torn knee ligament. To prevent further damage, I was instructed to wear a long knee strap, but it came with its own set of challenges.

My home was located on the third floor of a building with no elevator, and steep stairs stood between me and the ground floor kitchen. It was a daunting predicament. I didn't own a car, and even if I did, my mobility was severely restricted. The cost of the knee strap alone was a staggering $200, a daunting expense. I couldn't reach out to my coworkers because none of them had a car. They were also working as many overtime shifts as possible because, much like me, they were doing all they could just to survive. I felt utterly devastated, facing yet another formidable trial. In a world that often feels cutthroat, I knew I had to rely on myself to survive.

Driven by desperation, I turned to a dating app and messaged a man I had been chatting with for months. He had been wanting to meet for quite some time. In a bold leap of faith, I asked if he would meet me at the hospital, for I was in dire need. He responded with unwavering kindness and came to my aid. This young African man, a stranger to me until that moment, turned out to be my guardian angel. He helped me purchase the knee strap, carried me to his car, and transported me back home, even lifting me up those treacherous flights of stairs to my room. To my villa mates, it appeared as though he was my boyfriend, but I offered no explanation. He was a true instrument of God, sent to help me through my darkest hour.

As I navigated life with crutches, ordinary tasks took on an entirely new dimension of difficulty. Unlike in the United States, where grocery stores often provide grocery carts on wheels, Oman had no such thing. I found myself struggling, deeply empathizing with the challenges faced by those with disabilities. Each trip to the store required assistance, and I felt a profound sense of helplessness, isolation, and sadness.

But in the midst of this struggle, an extraordinary moment unfolded. An Indian woman named Lenny approached me and asked if I needed help. Tears welled in my eyes as I gratefully accepted her offer. Lenny, a Christian woman, explained that she rarely shopped at that store as it was far from her home. Yet, on that particular day, an inexplicable force drew her there. It was as if divine intervention had led her to me. She became like the big sister I had never had, offering her support and assistance during my time of need. To this day, I continue to pray for her and thank God for sending her into my life.

Reflecting on these moments, I am reminded of the famous poem Footprints in the Sand.

Mary Stevenson writes (1936):

> *One night, I dreamt I was walking along the beach with the Lord. Many scenes from my life flashed across the sky. In each scene, I noticed footprints in the sand. Sometimes, there were two sets of footprints. Other times, there was only one. The years when you have seen only one set of footprints, my child is when I carried you.*

In those moments when I felt abandoned, when all I could see were solitary footprints etched into the sand, my faith wavered, and I questioned whether God had forsaken me. The darkness of uncertainty crept in, casting doubt upon the path I was walking. I grappled with the sense of isolation and the heavy burden of life's trials, wondering why God had seemingly turned away.

It was during those very moments, however, as I now reflect upon the trials and tribulations I faced, that I've come to realize the profound truth—the one set of footprints I saw was not a sign of abandonment. Instead, it was evidence of God's unwavering presence in my life, a testament to His infinite love and care.

God, in His infinite wisdom, chose to reveal Himself through the most unexpected messengers—strangers who entered my life in serendipitous ways. These individuals, whether a kind-hearted soul from a dating app or a compassionate woman in the grocery store, became my unexpected angels. They were sent by divine providence to guide me through the darkest and most challenging hours of my life.

As I look back on these experiences, my faith in God has not only endured but has grown stronger. It remained steadfast, unwavering even in the face of adversity because I came to understand that God's ways are mysterious, and His presence transcends our understanding. His divine intervention was a constant force, quietly working behind the scenes to uplift me during my moments of greatest need.

These encounters served as a powerful reminder that we are never truly alone, even when life's trials threaten to overwhelm us. God's grace flowed through these strangers, demonstrating that His love knows no bounds and that He is always with us, carrying us through the most challenging and formative moments of our journey.

The footprints in the sand, those solitary marks in the moments of darkness, were not a sign of abandonment; they were a profound symbol of God's unwavering presence. They were proof that He walked beside me, carried me through the storms, and illuminated the path even when I couldn't see it myself. These footprints serve as a testament to the remarkable ways in which God's love and divine intervention shape our lives, turning trials into triumphs and adversity into opportunities for growth and faith.

PART IV

COPING WITH LIFE'S ULTIMATE TESTS

Death is the ultimate test of faith.

— GABRIEL KOCH

10

GRIEF COMES IN ALL COLORS— LIVING THROUGH LOSS

P icture it: The year was 2020, and the world was in the throes of the COVID-19 pandemic.

As I reflect upon that fateful year, it's impossible not to conjure up a vivid mental image of the world around me. It was a year that will forever be etched in my memory, a year that brought forth unparalleled challenges and heartaches for people across the globe. The COVID-19 pandemic had unleashed its relentless grip, causing waves of fear, uncertainty, and sorrow to wash over humanity.

I had been granted a precious vacation leave from my job, a break I eagerly planned to spend with my mother in the serene mountains of the Philippines.

My heart had swelled with anticipation in the days leading up to my long-awaited vacation leave. It was a respite I had been yearning for, an opportunity to temporarily cast aside the pressures of work and the demands of life abroad. My destination was the picturesque landscape of the Philippines, a country known for its natural beauty and the warmth of its people. But, more importantly, it was my mother's embrace that beckoned me home.

It was a rare opportunity for us to reconnect, to relish the natural beauty of our homeland, and to simply be together.

In the midst of the hustle and bustle of daily life, moments of pure togetherness had become increasingly scarce. The mountains of the Philippines, with their lush greenery and pristine air, offered the perfect backdrop for us to escape the demands of modernity and simply be mother and child once more. I yearned for the deep conversations, the shared laughter, and the silent understanding that only a mother and her child can share.

But fate had other plans, ones that I could not have foreseen.

The day before my departure back to Oman, where I had been working, an inexplicable sense of unease settled within the depths of my heart. It was a heaviness that refused to be ignored, a foreboding shadow that cast doubt upon the journey that lay ahead. As the hours of that restless night unfolded, my slumber was disrupted by

sweaty nightmares, each one more vivid and discon-
certing than the last.

A voice within me, a whisper from my Holy Spirit, grew
increasingly insistent, telling me that this might be the last
time I would see my mother.

Amid the disorienting realm of dreams, a voice—soft yet
undeniably authoritative—began to permeate my
consciousness. It was the voice of my Holy Spirit, an inner
guide that had often offered me solace and direction in
moments of uncertainty. On this night, however, its
message was hauntingly clear: "This might be the last time
you will see your mother."

It urged me to embrace her tightly, to express the depth of
my love, and to cherish every moment we had left.

I awoke in a cold sweat, my heart pounding with an inexplicable urgency. The message from the Holy Spirit
pierced the layers of my subconscious, leaving me with an
overwhelming sense of responsibility. It was as though
time itself had conspired to deliver a warning, urging me
to seize the moments that remained.

With a profound sense of purpose, I found myself driven by
an inner force. I knew what I had to do. I had to embrace my
mother to convey the love that often remained unspoken in
the hustle and bustle of our lives. I had to cherish every
moment, for I could no longer take them for granted.

This moment, this whisper from my Holy Spirit would prove to be a haunting premonition—a foreshadowing of the turbulent times and heart-wrenching losses that awaited me in the days, weeks, and months to come. It was a call to action, a plea to cherish the bonds of love while they still burned brightly before the shadows of grief would descend upon my world.

In the pages that follow, you will join me on a journey through these trials and tribulations as I navigate the profound losses that shook the very foundation of my existence. However, I resisted these thoughts, desperately clinging to denial. I couldn't bear to entertain the possibility that my mother's presence in my life could be extinguished. She had been my rock, my unwavering support, and the reason I had persevered through the challenges of life in a remote, impoverished part of the Philippines. In our earlier days, our home lacked running water and electricity, and we relied on the bounty of nature for our daily needs.

My mother had sacrificed so much to ensure my well-being. She had toiled tirelessly, working multiple jobs to put food on our table and send me to school. Her love knew no bounds, and in return, I had done everything in my power to provide her with the comforts and joys she deserved. I bought her a house with a garden, nurtured her green thumb with an abundance of plants, and facilitated her travels to more than ten different countries.

Through it all, she remained my greatest motivator, the driving force behind my every endeavor.

In the months leading up to the pandemic, I had shared with my mother my plans to resign from my job abroad and return to her side. We spoke casually about her desire for me to settle down and her hopes that God would bless me with a good Christian partner in life. Little did I know that these conversations would be the last we would share in person for the rest of my life.

As the COVID-19 pandemic tightened its grip on the world, I took a three-month unpaid leave from work, intent on traveling back to the Philippines to be with my mother. My heart ached with the desire to celebrate her 67th birthday in July, a momentous occasion that I didn't want to miss. But the world had changed, and restrictions and uncertainties now dictated our lives.

The day of my scheduled flight arrived, and I was filled with eager anticipation. However, fate had a cruel twist in store. Just as I was set to depart, the country imposed a ban on travelers from the Middle East, leaving me stranded. My plane ticket was refunded, and I found myself on a forced hiatus, unable to be by my mother's side during the pivotal moments of her life.

Despite the physical distance, I made every effort to stay connected with my mother. We spoke through video calls, and I eagerly assisted her in planning her birthday celebration from afar. I offered guidance on preparing her favorite dishes, like the tuna spaghetti I had taught her to make. I sent her extra funds to ensure her birthday party would be special, including a cake and ice cream. Her church friends joined in the festivities, and it brought her immense joy.

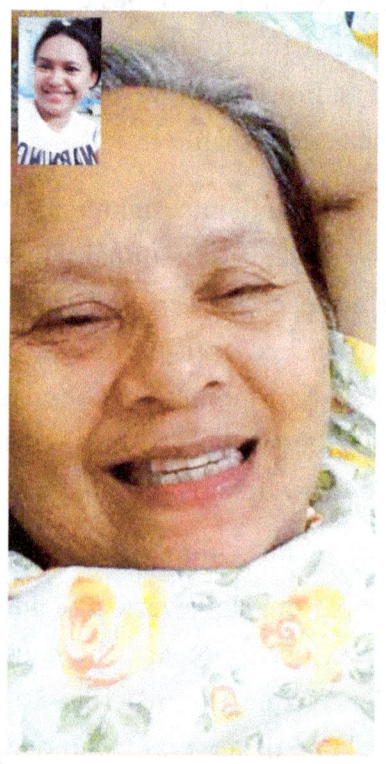

But just two weeks after her joyful celebration, my mother fell ill. What initially appeared to be a common flu quickly escalated into something far more sinister. She began to experience alarming symptoms—a bloated face, a distended stomach, and a persistent fever. Concerned for her well-being, I implored her to drink plenty of water and rest.

However, her condition continued to deteriorate, and as the pandemic surged, the local hospitals were overwhelmed. It was a dire situation, and we found ourselves in a race against time to secure medical care for her. My young nephew and niece, both minors, stepped up to care for her while neighbors aided us in delivering food. Our church community rallied around us, offering support as best they could.

It became a frantic struggle to find a hospital that would admit her. Her fever persisted, and it was clear that she needed urgent medical attention. We called every hospital in the area, even compiling a list in case a vacancy opened up. But the healthcare system was stretched to its limits, and many hospitals had no room for new patients.

As her condition worsened, my mother's breathing became increasingly labored. It was a harrowing experience to witness her suffering, unable to do anything to ease her pain. Desperation led us to seek out oxygen sources, as even this precious resource became scarce. A nurse friend of mine bravely stepped in to provide her with intravenous fluids, all while we fought to get her admitted to a hospital.

I was living a nightmare, trying to juggle the demands of my job with the urgent needs of my mother, thousands of miles away. Sleep eluded me, and I could hardly concentrate on anything other than the phone calls and messages that kept me tethered to her bedside. I was running out of leave days at work, and the financial strain added to the burden of my worry.

Throughout this ordeal, my young nephew and niece remained by her side, their unwavering devotion a testament to the strength of our family bonds. We begged hospitals to admit her, and there were moments when we believed we had found a lifeline, only to have it cruelly snatched away.

One heart-wrenching day, my mother was finally accepted into a public hospital, but her condition was dire. The precious oxygen she needed was in short supply, and she had to wait in the ambulance, gasping for breath, for four agonizing hours before she could be admitted. My heart ached as I watched her, helpless through the pixelated screen of my phone. The orange plush blanket she had intended to wash for her birthday had become her shroud, a cruel twist of fate that haunted me.

As her daughter, I felt a profound sense of guilt and help-lessness. I had surrendered everything to God, pleading for His will to be done while clinging to the hope of a miracle. But that hope was not realized, and on August 22, 2021, my beloved mother passed away.

The pain that engulfed me was unlike anything I had ever experienced. I was numb, in a fog of grief, unable to comprehend the enormity of my loss. My mother, my guiding light, my reason for being, had been taken from me. The world felt empty, and I was left with a void that nothing could fill.

The very foundation of my faith had been shaken. I was angry, bitter, and filled with questions. How could God, in whom I had placed so much trust, allow this to happen? My mother had been my constant prayer, my deepest wish, and yet her life had been cut short. I couldn't fathom why God had chosen to take her from me. My faith was shattered, and I felt betrayed.

In those dark moments, I questioned God's plan. How could He take her, the person I loved most in this world? The loss of my mother shattered me, and I felt like I had lost my anchor.

During all this, I had a fiancé, an Arab Christian Lebanese man who had met my mother and asked for my hand in marriage in person. We were planning for a life together for four years. But when my mother passed away, I didn't feel the support I needed from him. I still felt alone in my grief. I summoned the courage to ask him about our future, and his response was that he wasn't ready. At that moment, I realized that I needed to let him go, as painful as it was. It was four months after my mother's death, and the losses in my life seemed never-ending.

But the storm was not over. Just two months later, I lost my beautiful dog, Pretty, who had been my loyal companion for five years. The grief that had been haunting me continuously only deepened. It felt like I was drowning in sorrow, and I couldn't find a way to heal. My tears had run dry, and I was existing rather than truly living. I would burst into tears at random moments, overwhelmed by the weight of my losses. I felt utterly hopeless and questioned the purpose of my existence. I even found myself resenting God for taking everything I held dear.

Today, I share my story not as a tale of despair but as a testament to the strength that can be found in faith and the human spirit. I have learned that even in the face of unimaginable loss, there is a glimmer of light that can lead us out of the darkness. My journey is ongoing, and I continue to hold onto my faith in God as I navigate the twists and turns of life. Through it all, I have come to understand that faith is not the absence of doubt or pain but the ability to find hope and purpose even in the midst of our deepest trials.

11

GUIDED BY GRACE

Welcome to the pages of my life, where faith, divine intervention, and unwavering belief in God have played a central role in overcoming challenges and adversities.

My journey of faith began much earlier, at the tender age of three, in that rented room where I encountered a haunting presence. As I screamed for my mother, she introduced me to faith and God. She would recite Psalm 23 over and over, and I would close my eyes tightly, repeating the verses, feeling protected by God's embrace. It was in those terrifying moments that my faith took root.

I was just a young child, innocent and full of wonder when I found myself lost deep in the woods. The towering trees seemed to stretch endlessly into the sky, and the forest was an impenetrable maze. Panic surged through me as I realized I had no idea how to find my way back home. Tears welled up in my eyes, and fear gripped my heart.

In that moment of vulnerability, I turned to my faith. I remembered the verses of Psalm 23 that my mother had instilled in me. As I stood amidst the dense foliage, I closed my eyes, and with trembling lips, I began to recite those sacred words. "The Lord is my shepherd; I shall not want..." The verses provided solace and a glimmer of hope in the midst of my fear. Miraculously, a kind stranger soon stumbled upon me, guiding me safely back to my worried mother's arms. My faith had brought me comfort, and God's grace illuminated the path to safety.

High school can be a challenging time for anyone, but for me, it was a period filled with relentless bullying. Day after day, I faced taunts, ridicule, and the pain of exclusion because I was less fortunate than most. The weight of it all felt crushing, and I often questioned my worth and purpose.

During those trying years, my faith was my constant companion. In the solitude of my room, I would turn to prayer, seeking strength and courage to face each new day. I would remind myself that I was a child of God, worthy of love and respect. This faith-infused self-assurance helped me endure the torment and find the inner strength to rise above the cruelty of others. Gradually, the bullying subsided, and I emerged from that painful

chapter of my life with a deepened faith and an unwavering sense of self-worth.

College should have been a time of excitement and exploration, but it took an unexpected turn when I fell seri-
ously ill. Doctors couldn't immediately identify the cause
of my ailment, and I was gripped by uncertainty and fear.

I prayed for healing and strength, and I found solace in
the belief that God had a purpose for my life, even in the
face of illness. Miraculously, my health began to improve,
and I was able to continue my education. My faith had
carried me through the darkest hours of my illness and
had given me the resilience to rebuild my life.

Relocating to a foreign country brought new challenges
and dangers that I couldn't have foreseen. I found myself
immobilized and facing attacks from strangers and even
ex-boyfriends. The isolation and vulnerability I felt were
overwhelming, and it seemed like there was no way out.

Once again, I turned to my faith as my lifeline. In
moments of terror and desperation, I would fervently
pray for protection and guidance. I held onto the belief
that God was watching over me, even in the bleakest of
circumstances. Miraculously, I found the strength to
escape dangerous situations and seek help. My faith had
been my shield, guiding me towards safety and protecting
me from harm.

In all these moments, my faith was not a passive presence but an active force that sustained me. It was the unwavering belief that I was not alone, that a higher power was watching over me, guiding me through the darkest of times, and ultimately sparing my life. My faith, tested and strengthened by these trials, became an integral part of who I am today.

There were times when I was away in Oman, so far from my mother and family, that the isolation was unbearable. It was a sense of loneliness I can't put into words. Times my body would ache. Every time, God would send an angel to intervene. He sent Lenny to help in the grocery store. He sent a man from the dating app to help take care of me when I was immobile. I was always sent angels in many forms to help in the worst of times.

There were moments in my life when I couldn't help but question why God would allow me to go through such profound hardships. The loss of my dear mother was the most heart-wrenching experience of all. She had been my anchor, my source of unwavering love and support, and her absence left an immense void in my life. I couldn't understand why God would take her from me, especially when she had worked so tirelessly to provide for us.

In those moments of grief and loss, I felt abandoned by God. I was angry, hurt, and confused. I struggled to find meaning in the suffering I was enduring. It seemed as though the world had turned its back on me, and I couldn't see a purpose in my pain.

In the midst of my anguish, I embarked on a journey of healing and self-discovery. I needed to understand that death and life are intertwined, and loss is an inevitable part of the human experience. I realized that God wasn't punishing me; rather, He was inviting me to grow stronger through adversity.

It was during this time that I allowed myself to grieve fully. I embraced my pain and allowed myself to mourn the loss of my mother and other loved ones. I sought therapy and support from those who understood the depths of my grief. Through this process, I began to heal and grow. I discovered that my faith could coexist with my doubts and questions and that it was okay to feel anger and sorrow.

As I mentioned, there were moments when I lost my faith, when I questioned God's plan in the face of physical harm and emotional pain. It's natural to seek answers when life's challenges seem insurmountable. But through it all, I have come to understand that divine discernment is unshakable.

God's ways are not always clear to us, and His purpose may remain a mystery. However, I've realized that our faith can carry us through the storms of life. It's in those moments of doubt and uncertainty that our faith can become even stronger, like steel forged in the fires of adversity.

I've learned that God's plan is not always about sparing us from suffering but about guiding us through it. It's about the strength we gain, the compassion we develop, and the resilience we build in the face of life's trials. While we may not always understand why certain things happen, our faith can help us find meaning and purpose even in the midst of our darkest moments.

In essence, my faith has evolved from a simple refuge in times of trouble to a deep and abiding trust in God's divine plan, even when that plan remains a mystery. It's a faith that embraces both the highs and lows of life, and it's a faith that continues to sustain me on this remarkable journey of faith, growth, and resilience.

In sharing my story, I hope to inspire and uplift others who may be facing their own trials and tribulations. Life is filled with uncertainties, and we often find ourselves in situations where the path ahead seems shrouded in darkness. But I want to emphasize that it's okay not to have all the answers right away.

Hope is the beacon that guides us through the darkest of nights. It's the belief that, even when we cannot see the way forward, there is still a way. I have learned that hope can be found even in the most unexpected places, and it can flourish in the hearts of those who endure.

Resilience is the inner strength that allows us to bounce back from adversity. It's the ability to weather the storms of life and emerge stronger on the other side. We may not always understand God's message or the purpose behind our trials, but resilience allows us to keep moving forward, one step at a time.

Grief is a lifelong journey, and there is no set timeline for healing. Each person's experience of grief is unique, and it cannot be rushed or neatly packaged. It's essential to remember that there is no "right" path through grief. You must do what works best for you, at your own pace, and with the support that you need.

Allow yourself the space to grieve, to feel the pain, the anger, the sadness, and even the moments of peace and acceptance. Grief is not a linear process; it ebbs and flows like the tides. Sometimes, it may feel like you've taken a step backward, but that's okay. Healing is not a race, and there is no finish line. What matters most is the journey itself, the growth and transformation that can occur along the way.

Even in the darkest moments when you may feel abandoned by God, His grace is ever-present. It's a comforting truth that I hold dear to my heart. Divine grace is not contingent on our circumstances or our level of faith; it is a constant presence in our lives.

I am living proof that faith can light our way through the most challenging of circumstances. It's not about having unwavering faith at all times; it's about holding onto that glimmer of belief, even when the world around us feels chaotic and uncertain. Faith can provide us with the strength to persevere and the courage to face whatever lies ahead.

In closing, I encourage you to embrace your faith, whatever form it may take. It can be a guiding light in your life, a source of solace, and a wellspring of inner strength. Trust that your faith can and will guide you through your own journey of hope, healing, and unshakable resilience.

Remember that you are never alone in your struggles, and there is always hope, even in the darkest of times. As you navigate the challenges that life presents, may your faith be a constant companion, a source of comfort, and a testament to the enduring power of the human spirit.

CONCLUSION: A MESSAGE THAT ECHOES

In the quiet moments of reflection, as I sit here now, I can't help but marvel at the journey that brought me to this point. It's a journey that has been filled with hardships, challenges, and moments of despair, but it's also been a journey that has been marked by unwavering faith and divine intervention.

Picture it: the rugged mountains of the Philippines, where life was a daily struggle. My mother, a single parent, worked tirelessly to provide for our family, and despite the odds stacked against us, she instilled in me a deep belief in the power of education and the importance of faith in God.

I can still vividly recall those nights spent huddled over a rickety wooden table, with only the flickering light of a kerosene lamp to chase away the darkness. The winds outside would howl, threatening to extinguish that fragile flame, and the rain would patter relentlessly on our humble abode. But in those moments, I clung to my dreams like a lifeline. I knew that education was my ticket to a better life, and faith was the anchor that kept me from drifting away when the path ahead seemed impossibly steep.

Our journey didn't end in the Philippines. We embarked on many new chapters, and ultimately, I would end up in the Middle East, a place that felt worlds away from my familiar surroundings. Here, I became the family's sole breadwinner, working far from home and carrying the weight of my responsibilities on my shoulders. The sun blazed relentlessly, and the culture was vastly different from my own, but through it all, my faith in God remained my refuge, my guiding star in the darkest of nights.

As you've walked with me through the pages of this memoir, you've witnessed the moments when my faith was shaken to its core. Times when I faced danger and despair, and I wondered if God was truly there for me. But in those very moments of doubt, I found that God answered my prayers, sent angels to protect me, and revealed His love in profound and undeniable ways.

The losses I've endured—the heartbreaking passing of my mother, losing my fiancé shortly after, and the void left by the departure of my beloved dog—are wounds that still ache, scars that tell the story of battles fought and endured. Healing from such profound losses is a journey that continues, but through it all, I've come to understand that God wasn't punishing me. He was there to catch my tears, to hold me up when I couldn't stand on my own, to remind me that His love is unwavering, even in the face of unimaginable pain.

So, where do I sit with my faith now? I sit with it as a source of strength and comfort, a wellspring of hope that never runs dry. I lean into it every day, knowing that it was the beacon of hope that guided me through the darkest of times. My mother worked tirelessly so that I could have a better life, and for her, I will heal. For her, I will live a life of faith and devotion to God.

As I prepare to close this book of my life and the pages of this memoir, I want to extend my heartfelt gratitude to you for joining me on this extraordinary journey. Putting my story into words has been a challenging yet profoundly healing experience. My hope is that this memoir finds its way into the hands of those who need it most, those who may be facing their own trials and tribulations, so they, too, can find strength and inspiration in the enduring power of faith.

Remember, when it feels like there's only one set of footprints in the sand, you are not alone. You are being carried by a loving and ever-present God. I would like to ask you for a review in an attempt for this book to find its way to those who can draw strength and inspiration from my story, just as I have drawn strength from my faith and the unwavering love of those who have walked beside me on this remarkable journey.

With humble thanks.
E.T. Mulloney

REFERENCES

Cohen, L. (2019, January 26). *10 quotes about resilience for when life gets rough*. Talkspace. https://www.talkspace.com/blog/resilience-quotes/

Copel, S. (2020, July 9). *35 uplifting quotes to strengthen your faith in hard times*. Oprah Daily. https://www.oprahdaily.com/life/g33081629/faith-quotes/

Emberley, R. (2021, May 2). *Psalm 23: The message of the shepherd*. Greenfield Recorder. https://www.recorder.com/Faith-Matters-Emberley-40224274#:~:text=Psalm%2023%20reminds%20us%20that

Funny quotes about overcoming obstacles. (n.d.). Pinterest. Retrieved November 9, 2023, from https://www.pinterest.ca/pin/367747125802572586/

King James. (n.d.). *Psalms Chapter 23* . Www.kingjamesbibleonline.org. https://www.kingjamesbibleonline.org/Psalms-Chapter-23/

Koch, G. (2023, November). *Gabriel F.W. Koch quote: "Death is the ultimate test of faith."* Quotefancy.com. https://quotefancy.com/quote/2981481/Gabriel-F-W-Koch-Death-is-the-ultimate-test-of-faith

Stevenson, M. (n.d.). *Footprints in the sand* . Www.sapphyr.net. Retrieved November 12, 2023, from https://www.sapphyr.net/largegems/footprints.htm#:~:text=by%20Mary%20Stevenson%20(1922%20%2D%201999)

Wellman, P. J. (2015, December 23). *27 quotes about miracles*. Christian-Quotes.info. https://www.christianquotes.info/quotes-by-topic/quotes-about-miracles/

IMAGES

Property of E.T. Mulloney